From Milady's Wood

Scottish Contemporary Poets Series
(for further details of this series please contact the publishers)

Tom Bryan, *North East Passage;* 1 898218 57 9
Gerry Cambridge, *The Shell House;* 1 898218 34 X
Jenni Daiches, *Mediterranean;* 1 898218 35 8
Valerie Gillies, *The Ringing Rock;* 1 898218 36 6
William Hershaw, *The Cowdenbeath Man;* 1 898218 68 4
Brian Johnstone, *The Lizard Silence;* 1 898218 54 4
Anne MacLeod, *Standing by Thistles;* 1 898218 66 8
Ken Morrice, *Talking of Michelangelo;* 1 898218 56 0
Siùsaidh NicNèill, *All My Braided Colours;* 1 898218 55 2
Walter Perrie, *From Milady's Wood;* 1 898218 67 6
Maureen Sangster, *Out of the Urn;* 1 898218 65 X
Kenneth C Steven, *The Missing Days;* 1 898218 37 4

From Milady's Wood

Walter Perrie

SCOTTISH CONTEMPORARY POETS SERIES

SCOTTISH CULTURAL PRESS

First published 1997
Scottish Cultural Press
Unit 14, Leith Walk Business Centre
130 Leith Walk
Edinburgh EH6 5DT
Tel: 0131 555 5950
Fax: 0131 555 5018

British Library Cataloguing in Publication Data
A catalogue record for this book is available from the British Library

ISBN: 1 898218 67 6

The publisher acknowledges subsidy from the Scottish Arts Council
towards the publication of this volume

Printed and bound by
BPC-AUP Aberdeen Ltd

Contents

Walter Perrie was born in 1949 into the Lanarkshire mining village of Quarter to a family of Scots-Irish descent, though with seasonings from France and Wales. Six years at Hamilton Academy were followed by four in steelworks and local libraries before removing to Edinburgh where he took the MA in philosophy, supplemented later with the M.Phil. from Stirling.

He has travelled widely in Europe and in North America, writing five books of poetry, a collection of criticism, a travel book on Eastern Europe, as well as a quantity of uncollected literary and philosophical essays. He has also founded and edited various magazines, most recently as managing editor of *Margin,* an international arts quarterly.

For the past ten years he has made his home in the ancient Perthshire village of Dunning.

Acknowledgements

Versions of Thirteen Lucky Poems have appeared in *Spectrum* and in *Under Cover,* an anthology edited by Colin Nicholson for Shelter (1993).

From Milady's Wood

grant my ghost grace for this journey
so that my soul may unscathed cross
Battle of Maldon

and in the very core and navel of the wood
there seemed a vacuum, if you stayed quite
still, as though you'd come on ancient
stillnesses in his most interior place.

David Jones
In Parenthesis

I

F and High G

Pi-leu, pi-leu a redshank pipes
pi-leu, pi-leu, a shingle shore
a note of love, a note of grief
clean on the ebony water.

II

To Egan O'Rahilly
for James Merrill

At last the hazel fruits have fallen. The fish
that slow, cold salmon in its bloodless pool
may now be taken, cooked and eaten
shared by an oak-fed fire before we go
among our wilderness of bog and money
elevated and witless as Suibhne
wandering.

It may be O'Rahilly, that the ignorant
have finally won – as may be they ought!
That Valentine Browns shall reign for ever
while you and I – that have McCabe and Creihen
in my lines – weighty with ancient rubble
be heaved briskly into oblivion's
wide-mouthed bog.

When the fervent souls of a fevered world
howl in unsacramental violence
when the West forgets again everything
imagination craves, remember the light
in a broken glen and the bountiful
voices wild in their measure, their chorus
of blessing.

When only the craft is left, O'Rahilly,
when only the arrogant craft remains
for testing our testament and truth
when all that is breakable is broken
mind me through dumbness, despair, forgettings
with airs and your murmured orderings
Brightness of Brightness
returning.

III

Moulted the woodlands now to their autumn plume
and swifts all in a whirl have shed their lethal young.
For a moment, untensed by appetite or dream,
we too delay departure and from north-west scan
southward the full-drawn bow of islands breasting
a placid Monet-coloured Minch, acknowledging
their ardent gift, though even here the uproar
of a toy-size tractor furrows the limpid air.

The sky glows pallid as a vacant TV screen.
Invisible a spirited songthrush asserts
his repertoire of territory, tribe or season
across a moor where song once gave to human hearts
heart's ease. Neglected now, infield and outfield, house
broken, stories scattered like their tellers below
bracken and whin, foundations a nest for the field-mouse
and where grief shared a smoking hearth-side, thistles grow.

> *This hearth, tall brambles cover it.*
> *Easy were its ways.*

> *This hearth, dockleaves cover it.*
> *More usual upon its floor*
> *mead, and the claims of men who drank.*

> Tacksmen and tenants all
> are fled the carnival.
> Empty are hearth and hall
> broken the bond.

Pale, shivering islands, broken glens, did not protest
the emptying of their people out, not Mull
not Islay nor the Angus Braes. Strathnaver washed
its hands of them in burning blood. So they went, vengeful
or hopeful, pious, secreting their pride and stories.
But every silent clachan, harbour, field or dun
waits each night its tale of parting, bitter glories
and the pain of immemorial habitation.

IV

A swaggering *Conundrum* struts from the ceilidh
hall, stepping out over the sussurant Sound
diffusing into imperceptibility.
Away from the music and blustering lights we stand
looking up to the blaze in a frosting sky
selves present, lost and alight in its spectacle
affirming the timely limits of the eye
knowing most of what is, is invisible.

Limit is not some uncrossable sea, only
a chilly highland burn spilling from a deep cleft,
virginal. And near its source one step would do
for translation, though the weight we have to lift
beyond blood and bone is heavier than God's. Easy
enough for stag, salmon, hound or otter, theirs
is a careless crossing lightly to territory
they have always known. We alone reap the despairs

of lives unlived, hopes unanswered, dreams undone.
Hunter and hunted, conspiracies in innocence
may hurt the heart but the enduring Cuillin
crumbles on the enigma of a future tense
and we, the least knowing, are the least translatable
element in all we say, our meaning obscure
and dim with doubt and no more than a mouthful
of spirit for comfort against this questioning air.

V

Not from the promontory, headland or raised beach
but low from out the fragments frost and gale have prised
from their high stations, as the gossiping gods pitch
dice or bones, ruthlessly hence to be revised
by current usage, all earth's crimps and proverbs scoured
blank. Edges are always precarious, none more
than here between fixture and fluency, unsecured
foot-slithering, shape-shifting, storm-battered border.

October month and its insistent westerlies
scours the landscape, stripping woods back to their structure
as age and stress one day across a cousin's face
unveiled, heart-stoppingly, a glimpse of our grandfather.
So why be astonished when they abandon you,
words and the shiny passions you once thought your own?
They always hankered for the anonymity
of crowds, never shared your feelings of possession.

Out on the open water, barges and from the darkness
voices, distant, indistinguishable monotone
rehearsing the story, all the ancestors wish
us into Being, resent us never having been.
All the words that went before me, all their lives
converge like stars condensing to create a space
for speech, still stumble-speaking out against the waves'
nonsensical uproar and their infidelities.

VI

for Jack Sloan

Eye-weary tired I squint into the fire
till slip from out its flame a host of spears
shifting, darting brightnesses and I remember,
wedged tight into a window-seat forty years
before, beside parents smelling of rain-
damp winter coats, squinting into street lights
to revise our bus-ride as an alien
caravan trekking far from the Sunday night's
call on grandparents and a grandmother who,
a century ago, stood in her firelit
room in Keady and through the big-house window
gazed and sent her candle-splintered blaze out
across the closing menace of the park,
spearpoints piercing the vivid Irish dark.

VII

She Who Was The Helmet-Maker's Beautiful Wife

'*Grotesqueries,* monstrosities,
Balzac, the Good Burghers, now this
nothing escapes his deforming hand!'

Shoulders and the large head are bowed,
hair a limp straggle, eyes sunken
as the cheeks, shank and the thigh bone
thin as a wrist, two flaccid sacs
for breasts, the belly a prolapse,
her bent body a semaphore
for misery, age and labour.

But from beneath luminous bronze
a ghost still flickers through her bones,
thick hair to tangle husband's hand,
red cheeks to tell of sun and wind
caress, taut slopes of belly rise
to high breasts, fall away to thighs
strong to cradle and in her eyes
such confidence of self-belief...
what could cloud her gaze, she who was
the helmet-maker's beautiful wife?

VIII

Ithaka

September's louche disfigurations
gather in brittle crowds below
acacia and olive tree as
swallows put on their good-bye show.

Penelope, her tacit fingers,
warped with their telling at the loom,
gathers in knotted walnut hands
the folds of her bridal costume.

Brisk whirr and click of the cicadas
ebbs and a blessed sea breath cools
Ithaka's fever as daylight fades
from the tapestry's tale for fools.

'A world unravels and the ploy
is done. Let Ithaka have its charade
and me grow old. But tell me boy,
who is that beggarman there in the shade?'

IX

Ignorant of song or story to belong to
past and the future mumble in autistic trance
and we, uncertain, abandoned, must each say
our riddle: who we are, why now, why here and silence
our worry. Without us the story is helpless
as we are. Without an adventure to bless
it, the shining Minch is mere water, the thrush song
mechanical, our peace precarious porcelain.

Grousecalls – *goback goback goback* – Day cools, the slope
turns treacherous in a tricksy dusk. Tall shadows
hazel, rowan, rock put on old shapes and slip
away. The cool white lady of the moon glows
on the Cuillin. An age that fears blessing and curse
alike cries its domestic fables, tunes for the purse
as twilight graces its airs for aisling and vision.

Fantastic hopes that truth be whatever we wish
that every well-meant belief be equally true
shatter, snail shells on the thrush's rock, and crash
and groan of a wild man-drowning Minch is only
a sough of history's unhappiness. Sunset.
Now as the waiting spirits strike their gongs and crow
to call the next batch of their bodies home, let
the little self go free to the patient indigo.

X

Hearing the Sluagh in Milady's Wood (I)

We cannot get lost in the ordinary wood,
it is not wide nor wild enough to beguile
our senses and we see nothing reflected
in its eyes but our bodies made simple.
That wood has no centre, only a boundary
where the pheasants shine and our misery
prowls like the fox whose bark at morning echoes
its isolation down the oaks and beeches.

But deep in the dangerous wren-smitten wood
centred, imageless, unwilling, unwilled
a stillness waits while old in pride and cunning
we worry our world, for its profit and passion.

> Along the wood's familiar paths
> lie secret ways and hidden raths.
> Where did you go when you went away?
> *Down the blood into futurity.*

Only the trill of the wren, an abandon
of Being, only the clatter of pigeon wings
only the sapling's unstated oration
only the in-between silences waiting...

Harping, harping out of the sapient axil
a stillness, harmonies fragile as blossom
stirring, till air-strung bows of birch and hazel
strike earthly spells and a summoning rhythm.

Harping, harping and a flute-breath mossy green
burgeoning from stillness and the other wood,
its eyes alight for summoning, dreams the wren
to bless the story, strip it of vanity and falsehood,
guide us. He is not shy the darting wren-lord
dancing always a little before us close
to the earth. Rather, we fear his angered word
strip us to suddenly shivering nakedness.

Wary we follow him into uncertainty
and the long-thorned thicket, hoping some antidote
for a failing heart may flourish on the tree
he sings from, unwithering, inviolate,
warded by silence from our indefatigable
want, the endless howl of hurting hunger.
Harrow the pheasant and the fox to death, in thrall
to loss, we haunt the surface of an injured mirror.

Greedy gods our cacophonous days consume us
leaching us thinner and thinner till the *ingenu*
parches to con-man or pedant, dying of loss, loss
of remembrance that we also belong here, we too
are, for all our confusions, real and a mirror
for stillness, for wren-song, for visions to shine in
burnished as sunlight burnishes still water,
endlessly full as the marvellous cauldron.

XI

Flint

Hieratic wood glosses the ploughland's limit
a buzzard pair spirals on porcelain
a tractor grumbles, pale earth turns russet
as the share inscribes its orders line by line.
The turnings at the furrow's end are measure,
earth versed for her assonantal barley, wheat
or whatever we study to spell there
in elemental auspices of wind, rain, heat:

slender-tongued, a willow-leaf arrowhead
exacting its angles of revelation,
hunting tool, fable and weapon quarried –
poised, elegant as any Mondrian –
to purely human announcement, icon
cut from the geological babble
taciturn obduracy fiercer than steel
water-fed silicate, chalcedony-like
a knapped flint by step-flake and feather-edge,
conchoidal fractures, calculated strike on strike
exhumed, ink-lustrous to its fresh-ploughed page.

XII

Hearing the Sluagh in Milady's Wood (II)

Swelling through the wood's broad belly the constant
purr of rain, a growling almost and the taste
of a sudden earth-scent. Lughnasa and faint
through the wide-pillared nave of beeches a gust
of voices, noises swelling jingle and clop
of harnessed horses, croak of ox-carts and groan
of great bull horns, clarion carnyx and step
of multitudes moving in slow procession.

Down the shaded aisle approaching, no twig breaking
riding or marching, banner-bearing, an army
    Shouting for battle
fluent as water and swathe of life slaking
a thirst for fate. And as they flow before me
through me grim faces dapple-stain to shadow
    Though they were slain they slew
    none to his home returned.
each on his narrow road for Camlann, Catraeth, Badon
fosse or field or moorland hillock and a glow
of bloody sunset staining Dupplin Braes or Flodden.
    After the war-cry, bitter the grave.

Silent glide of the lethal owl is less unkind
than we with our passion for causes and heroes,
infecting whole continents, a pest wind
bred in the shallows of our three consuming woes;
loyalties and faiths and sorrows, as if each Good
mutated its peculiar wickedness
with no immunity. But in the silly Wood
the pale contingents of the centuries still pass.

Four abreast now, ranks in rhythm, each man helmeted
for safety, stepping out for France or Flanders'
beaux paysages, obedient as lovers led
on in their dreaming down to a grey dawn at Wipers.
    Commoner was blood upon the grass
    than the plough in fallow land

Many the women they widowed
many the mothers who wept.

Magical and faded banners call their roll
of tattered names: Tobruk, Salerno, Dunkirk, Arnhem
famous victories for someone, confusion's toll
of kin-blood paid from Singapore to Alamein.
        Sleeps now the wide host of Caledon
        with the light in their eyes.

Still now, sea-cry and battle-boast fall still.
Ceremonial as sentries the woodlands wait
as our own contingents, tail-end charlies, straggle
south to slouch or swagger to their chill salute.
        No more the well-trained horses
        no more the scarlet cloaks...
        chill my legs, bare, uncovered.

These shall be our Unremembered, vagrant host
of youths and maidens, cynical innocents
streetwise and brutal, knowing no temenos
nor task, serving no cause, condemned to the trench-
war of a city-maze, threadless to face
no bloody bull-god but a heart-consuming ghost
subtle, invisible. These are the sacrifice
down and out on our luck, trolling the wide waste
        lands of Piccadilly
        for fifteen quid, a friendless fuck
        and a weeping room in Hackney.

        Cynddylan's hall is dark tonight...
        I weep awhile, and then am still

        brothers who grew like hazel saplings
        all are gone, one by one...

        Cynddylan's hall is dark tonight
        no fire is lit, no candle burns
        God will keep me sane.

Such is the dowry we, loaf-wards and ring-givers,
bequeath the children of the supple wood
gift of our feasting and silences, falsehood
and greed: ignorance and cardboard shanties, rivers
tainted, woods defiled, houses and speech bone-bare
of memory, of song and no-one to share
out the story for no city-grown tree grows high
enough to let them climb through and into the sky.

Ignorant and empty-handed we enter
the wood, lured by our thirst for its nourishing dark,
not promised happiness, only a stillness more
piercing than blackthorn as the wood weighs our heart
against, on its own confession, say, a pigeon feather
floating past. Perilous then to crack the stillness
as the wren passes his judgement on our grammar
of hurt and hope and a low wind soughs in the grass.

> In the near fields a tractor
> and the young fierce as ever.
> What persists is obscure
> but continuous.
> And what do they die for
> the generations?
> To be in the stillness of the wood
> still in the Great Wood of Caledon.

XIII

Ancestors

Her hands were walnut
his ivory pale.
From their gentling grip
I could never fall.

Beneath the lamp's hard glare
my hands, delicate remote
as jade seem unaware
what blemishes denote.

Walnut, ivory, jade
strip down to clap their praise
abandoning quietly rings
to engraving's paraphrase.

XIV

Crete – a fragment

No matter what Theseus felt or thought, what private
passion closed his eyes, cupped hand and ear to whisper
'dare' and guide him through his enterprise. Enough that
he was there-then ready to die and answer
for the tyrant story, to adventure out
among its endings as their hero, monster, lover.

In another wood on a sun-swept hillside
in the sweat of noon the young men prance
their bull-dance still, arms high, their heads nod
in the heavy masks and white dust, dense
as plaster, coats their legs. Only the dead
can be reborn, remade for their dying audience.

Timbre of stricken bronze and prophecy
among the rustling oaks where the women wait
stoic and silent, withdrawn from the dancers. Do
not believe because you are dying the light
dies with you: lovers, as earth to the plough,
rise like a blade to the blossoming throat.

XV

Monsieur Renoir

Ancient anti-Semite, bigot and snob
denouncing loudly to the whole café
'that traitor Dreyfus' mocking to the mob
old, ill Pissarro as 'the Wandering Jew'

Arthritic fingers twisted back
upon the wrist, his thumb askew
the skin so sensitive a hack
will open if he holds a brush
without some cushioning of silk.
Obsessive, desperate to flesh
out canvas with the dreamy bulk
of progenitive brown women.

And to the insolent question
'How can you paint with hands like those?'
art's laboured flowering in his gaze –
avec ma queue!

XVI

Spirit lamp flares, the last of the tunes has put away
its dancers and the stumbling heroes have gone
home to sleep it off. From spirit light and sleepy
dark other dancers, voices start their conversation
with my ancient loves, rooms, injuries again.
Sleep and the dead people the rath we rise from
into procession where ours is the matter of meaning
and speech, sane or wild, is all that remains us of home.

And the Wood, forever at its fall, still waits for us,
we who have hardly forgotten enough yet
to live with its mundane wonders and fabulous
things, grey-lichened rock, the rain, unspeakable light.
Before the step down again to the greenwood rath
and hidden kingdom, forgetting my grammar
for ancestral tongues and a bodiless truth
trope and a measure must pardon my pause here.

Equalities of abstract moment measure out
unequal dreams, our metronome, a chronic liar
tick-tocks its way from *is* to *seems,* we hyphenate
twin darknesses with *never yet* and blank *before.*
And no mask is forbidden us, impersonal
in solvent death we catalyse dream and myth
to crystal forms of mortal mess, alchemical
tales exchanging us for heroes with our dying breath.

Poor Oedipus, forever at his cross-roads
forever to answer and forever doomed.
Beguiling us with our success the doubtful gods
heap up their gifts and we, entranced as infants, groomed
and polished, dressed up for our outing never guess
the rocketing price of the party, blinded,
lame to stumble out on pathless roads the pythoness
decrees in oracles ambiguous as wind.

The world is not ordered as we half believed,
times and our wishes roll the world-circling sea
wherein our loves and losses are forever grieved,
forever green, forever swept in a propinquity
of ancestors and chance encounters, speech and pain,
each soul bound to its people by a gossamer
more binding than carbon, enduring than heaven
in tapestries of earth and water, light and air.

XVII

The Wild Geese Return

Grey mist cancels the village
concealing the circling hills.
Under its shallow sky
the houses huddle closer
and somewhere
circling geese cry and cry…

The story is also dream:
cradle-song, love song, hymn
work-song, incitement, lament
boundary stones, ancestral
and somewhere
circling geese cry and cry.

Grey mist cancels the village
shrouding the path behind
as ever ahead we scry
phantoms of happiness
and somewhere
circling geese cry and cry…

Neither wish nor the story
proffers the longed-for gift,
asepsis, life without hurt
and mess of the mortal
and somewhere
a mountain hare screams
and the geese cry and cry.

Grey mist cancels the village
each cry muffles a question.
The pavements will not reply
with footstep notation
and somewhere
circling geese cry and cry…

the mist is autumn's changeling
as story, wish and song
are changeling human children
circling where we belong
and somewhere
a mountain hare screams
and the geese cry and cry.

XVIII

The Wood is

patient for felling by limber
young men, mere acres of timber
so many percent per annum
return on a capital sum...

trumpet bright for a chanterelle
pale for the destroying angel
buzzing certainty of the bee
light on mortal tongue like honey...

for ever just beyond our reach
analphabet of subtle speech
text for the gnostic scholiast
index of all our bless and blast.

XIX

Picking the Plum

September leaves drip crystal from the bush
plum. Under each freighted branch a blush
of sleek fruit, pendant gold and violet.
I twist one from its spur, my sleeves all wet.

A wasp has hollowed out an eighth-inch bowl,
one twist of knife excises all her trouble.
Just large enough to see without a glass
on sweet wet flesh her single egg in place.

Days of long warm light turn into sugar
on the tongue and I and not a future
wasp am filled, chipping the naked stone,
still clutching its kernel, onto the garden.

Though alternative fates may not puzzle
plumtree or wasp or the summer drizzle,
no myth nor mystery is hidden here:
in plain view one world is become an other.

XX

Dunning Funeral
I.m. J. S. Wilson

Dark ribbon the mourners, mostly men
winds along the street and square
trailing the flagrant coffin
and crumples at the gateway where
village and our service ends.

Cold seeps through soles and the folk subdued
as trees this January day
black, exposed we wait bare-headed
to file the cemetery pathway's
short road ridged with frozen mud.

The stones here are relatively new.
In the old yard, all fallen together
lichen-crusted with the authority
of crumbling things the incisions are
ciphers, blank for irony

flaking, the old red sandstone
upright for something illegible
past all mind or minding what has been
or ever will.

On the very rim of the village
the green strath waits to be given
into her broad minded pasturage,
to the long and lovely Strath of Earn,
heart and the body's homage
guarded by Voirlich and Stuc a' Chroin.

XXI

Tracings on Glass

That's settled then, one summer together before
we take our inter-leaving passages:
drive to Loch Earn or round by Callander
for high September's pyrotechnic braes,
pass lazy evenings seat by seat listening
to your histories of the bad-old-days
and he shall play harmonica and sing
ballads long since confined to libraries.

I glimpsed myself as in a glass
reflecting in the morning light
such after-images of dream
as though those years had still to pass
their gifts and losses never been
and you both still in your habits
       brown and green.

O in a stillness of deceit
to catch the wholly world off-guard
surprise the uninvited guest
with what we trace upon the glass –
       wishes or lies?
while cataracting transformation
       clouds the eyes.

XXII

Some Night

Some night she will wait
    on a windy moor
        for me
    to answer her
the tall white woman
    of my people.

Juniper berries are bitter
grouse berries are sweet
and the Sidhe to their hosting
ride on silent feet.

Thirteen Lucky Poems

celebration and requiem

You, sometimes will lament a lost friend,
for it is a custom:
This care for past men...

Ezra Pound
Homage to Sextus Propertius

Departure I

leavetaking

Failing lovers
drinkers at dawn
cafés
under this tyranny
these unacknowledged
vanishings
stumble
one by one
signlike
towards vacancy.

Return I

miracle

Though frost through five
nights has thickened its gelid crust
the burn swings on
shadowy minnows a-flitter
in unison.

Hot coffee by the hissing fire
and the bland voice exhausting dire
events across four continents;
how many died, how many may expire.

Biscuit-dry crisp
hills under snowy icing
and ptarmigan
crackle and yap, whurr from the sight
of the human.

Read Hume *On Miracles* again.
Misanthropy is easy when
abstraction and unlovely fact
exhaust the love-lost citizen.

On the high tops
in the deep deer-sheltering glens
weak things totter
and the hungry dipper baffled
walks on water.

Departure II

Fine-grained as though duration
were density the image
records each light-carved detail:
legendary doors ajar
and inter-twining angels
tenth-century bishops
gargoyle heads, early Saints –
who may have existed or not.
As though duration were density
in extended exposure
the flitting crowds are gone.

Return II

Presence why do you hide so
for ever skip hopping
from word to word your cuckoo
calling always stopping
when I think I have you?

Why so skilfully obscure?
It is a con, a shame
at some wound or want in our
tryst – or a stupid game
without meaning or cure?

Or do I slyly exile
you fearfully greedy
for some phantasy to wile
out death ever needy
of new woods, another style?

Whimsical as a cuckoo
you vanish for days, years
till, all at once, peek-a-boo
you assaulting my ears.
Presence why do you hide so?

Presence, Presence have I guessed
how you find your victim's nest –
between hope and hurt a secret place
thorny as life and thin as grace?

Departure III

after Hokusai

Skewed line of the ruled pine
leaning back from an edge
hides a triangular
terror – pine, rider, horse
poised upon emptiness.

Where we have paused to look
there is nothing to see
nothing below our crag
but purple abyss and
celebratory snow.

The horse bows down his head
knowing the rider's face
is turned away too tired
of the poems he can
not love or abandon.

Sound souls asleep in
dry taciturn houses
we are abandoned by
will not miss us. Morning
will have covered our tracks.

Rider and horse withdraw
from sadness to go on
fording white spaces where
we may not follow them
through their maidenly snow.

Return III

April

Dominican
peeweeps
sweeten
their earth again.

Oyster-catchers
beat a piercing
way up river and in
the guttering
snowmelt
morning
a pair of sparrows
polkas.

Departure IV

Foam-fingered
greedily
green waves
reach
for me
and the dragon
thin with dancing
high above
remembered
mountains.

Return IV

Through plum
stain windows
sun sweet
plovers
rise from foam.
What is there not
to celebrate?

Departure V

traditional after Hokusai

By the balcony
        The moon is out
my friend looks back
        for hearts fishing
to invisible homes
        boats are leaving
forbidden
        harbour and pine
exile
        is gripping earth
loss
        hard
          and far away.

Return V

A small rain settles in to Creag nan Gabhar
drawing the skies down, stirring the ember
moss to brightness, hitching a faded haar
     more tightly to her shoulders
     till from the cloud and drowsing boulders
     nine regal does come trotting
down, indian-file to their peat-black pool
and wait, alert, immobile, not drinking.

Unmoving I wait, breathing slowly, wait
     crouched in the heather, sodden
     chilled. The curlews are silenced, the spate
     of the earth-brown burn inaudible.

     What are we waiting for? But still they
     wait till the hillside shivers
     numbly forgetting to exhale.

     Then I see, half-see him through the haar
albino stag, almost invisible.

Departure VI

artless armoured
innocents mortal
we
adventured out
to track
down dragonish
mystery

our selves
stalked stalled
capricious
you solo
precede me

blatant now
the facts
of being
conscious
physical
going to die
are more
than mystery
enough

Tenebrae

The once umbilical places severed
look littler now than remembered confusing
loftier eyes with unmeaning loss.
The stones are stones and sward and whin
disguise themselves behind loneliness.
No man steps in the same stream twice.
Questing waters trickle or spate at flaw
and crack in the widening sense of limit
as the silt in the heart's channel shifts.
We are not large enough to contain our dying.
Smoother, lighter than any liquid
it assumes our shaping sadness to define
all we failed in becoming as goal
and origin exclude all but skeletal
prehension.

A tense imperfect is our tributary
glossing our glories out over the lip
of a fall, out into prismatic light.
Whatever provocation flaw and foible
can solicit from nothing kneads us
moulding their definite conduit and course
hurtless as the gift of pain. What we are
good at is suffering, not on behalf
of anything but quantum by quantum
inventing loss unthinking why the heart
behaves so badly. None of our numbers
count what we inflict on water nor tongues
name what we foil and foul. What's given
only osmoses back into earth-stuff
and silence.

Thinking of you now and all we were not
I should put out honey and oatbree
to sweeten the throats of our shadows.
This is no place for forgiveness their thirst
has still to be sated and we to become
selflessly fluent in otherness.
O spirits help us to bear the straining
syntax of water shape-shifting as
with absolute authority autumn
places a blue spear straight through the heart.
The easy part is the resigning
art of tumbling into the letterless
blue far out and high above the wrinkling shore
where sea and sun circle as eagles and
soar soar soar.

Kells

praise on praise
curlicue forest
faces peer from
page on page
labours asleep
like seed o
in bird woven
branches bold
with berries
calling
to morning
translate me
eat me out
of this marriage
to old skins
better abandoned

angel and animal
stacked
in our stories
wait for
a reader
patient
to flutter and stump
from crypts where scripts
are encrypted
from cells
to suns
drunk over
an O or the L
of a bell
summoning
lover

Three versions

Pause, reader, give thought
to what I am brought;
earth covers my eyes
my feet will not rise
in the dance again
as they once did down
long-suffering earth.

after Muhammad Banu Zuhr of Cordoba

La rose du monde entier
n'est pas pour moi.
Pour moi seulement
la rose de mon pays
petite et blanche
si parfumée de douce douleur
percer le coeur.

after MacDiarmid

Animula

So, little soul, you fleet away,
companion-sharer of my clay.
Where will you go; some darkling place,
anonymous, wanting the grace
that dappled our togetherness,
our happy laughter and our laughing play?

after Hadrian

For Gabrielle de Bohun

Old? Yes, simplified to mechanical
measures of heartbeat, and the weary bone
nods like a metronome and tyrannical
time agrees; you *are* old. But the saxophone
insidious as love insists; Not So,
the heart has other measures and the bone
can still keep time to ragtime tunes, the tiptoe
kiss enflame a fierce imagination.

Fragments there are but no fractions of beauty.
Though time may hurt us till our pleasures ache,
time cannot measure by how much we die
nor niggard out our care by clock-tick
and somewhere in the dark house of the soul
a child still wants a light on in the hall.

Shorts

The mirror alters year by year.
Faces I once knew as my own
now disappear into a where
not even memory may go.

* * *

Those weights are the greatest that nothing weigh,
unbalanced nothings, desire and duty.

* * *

The heart has no glimmer
of clock-tick or the play
of stars. Its calendar,
decades blank, keeps only
its ancient mysteries,
grandmother's certainties
a first love's death, a dream,
sweep of the scythe in Autumn.

* * *

Some among my ancestors
though they wielded shield and sword
understood that heaven's doors
only ever open inward.

* * *

Should I have half forgotten you,
being old or mad or worse,
some blameless evening you will walk
smiling into my memory
as though our crazy, bitter talk
had never ended and the curse
of our desire was all we knew.

Rations

Fame's thin gruel to sup on
Power bids you feast alone
Wealth buys a richer coffin
how then ought poets dine?

Why claws and rime for starters
and hard-boiled hearts for meat
sugared follies in a dish
uncritically sweet.

Merlin (I)

Nephew, this cave sucks almost as much as
your century. Now pass me your comb, my
beard's like a bramble – too long on my ass

glossing conundra! So you'd like to try
your wits on magic, potions, spells and all
that guff. What fun – someone to edify!

You and your fellows have come a long haul
since days a pinch of saltpetre would scare
off marauders or merchants, an obol

would get me to Hades and poor trouvères
still got a better press than racketeers.
A long haul and still more of a danger

to enemies, friends and co-planeteers
than ever, with no hint of a sense of scale
or proportion. Your antics would bring tears

to a marble eye and the grim detail
of your doings better unsaid. Techné,
shazzam! that childish obsession the male

of the species displays for unholy
gadgets, smart cards, clever bombs and his faith,
fundamental, strong on stupidity.

No wonder the angels and dragons with
drew to safe distance. You thought you'd driven
the Dark Ones out, reduced to comic myth

the monsters, only to feel your cold skin
crawl at some filthy thing squirming deep in your
own dark well. It's not brutality, sin-

ful enough, nor sheer numbers that colour
this age as distinctive – Timur the Lame
was no slouch at a shambles – but the sour-

as-bile, ice morality in whose name
you excuse yourselves. Perhaps to the dead
it's all one and suffering has the same

limit in any language, or blood shed
is but a bloodless fantasy to us,
the uniquely fanatical biped.

I shouldn't read Marcus Aurelius!
He makes me dyspepsic. Enough! Magic?
It's all a sort of magic, dangerous

in apprentice hands.

Notes

From Milady's Wood

To Egan O'Rahilly
Valentine Brown is a figure of mockery in O'Rahilly's great poem *A Grey Eye Weeping*. *Brightness of Brightness* is the usual English title for his aisling poem.

Section III
The quotations are from Llywarch Hen's *Elegy for Urien.*

Section VII
A cast of the bronze can be seen in Glasgow's City Gallery.

Hearing the Sluagh (2)
The Sluagh is a hosting of the Sidhe.
Milady's Wood is the local name for what appears on the maps as Kincladie Wood. Dupplin estate where the battle was fought in 1332 is about three miles from Dunning.
The quotations are from the early Welsh *Elegy for Geraint,* Aneirin's *Gododdin,* the Cynddylan poet, Taliesin and Llywarch Hen.

Flint
With appropriate synchronicity, a few weeks after I completed the poem, a Mesolithic flint scraper was found just on the northern edge of the village.

The Wild Geese Return
In heavy mists the geese will not land and sometimes circle the village for hours, all the time calling out to each other, invisible.

Thirteen Lucky Poems

The sequence commemorates a painter friend. Though I have long admired Hokusai, some of these poems draw on particular Hokusai prints and paintings, especially *A Mirror of Chinese/Japanese Verse,* published posthumously in 1853–4, a central theme of which is the exile of many of the classical poets.

Departure III
A Mirror, Chinese Poet in Snow.

Departure IV
Dragon Above Mt. Fuji, 1849 and signed *Old Manji in 90th year.* In later life Hokusai often signed pieces Old Man Mad With Painting.

Return IV
Fuji at Sea, 1835.

Departure V
A Mirror, The Poet Nakamaro in China.